Charities –
do they work?

Alison Brownlie

WAYLAND

Talking Points series

Alcohol
Animal Rights
Charities – do they work?
Divorce
Eating Disorders
Family Violence
Genocide
Homelessness
Mental Illness
Slavery Today

Editor: Jonathan Ingoldby
Series editors: Alex Woolf / Jason Hook
Designer: Simon Borrough
Production controller: Tracy Fewtrell
Consultant: Neil Jones, Communications Director, Charities Aid Foundation

First published in 1999 by Wayland Publishers Ltd, 61 Western Road, Hove, East Sussex BN3 1JD, England

Find Wayland on the Internet at
http://www.wayland.co.uk

British Library Cataloguing in Publication Data
Brownlie, Alison
Charities: do they work? - (Talking points)
1. Charities - Moral and ethical aspects - Juvenile literature 2. Charities - Political aspects - Juvenile literature 3. Charities - Economic aspects - Juvenile literature
I.Title
361.7

ISBN 0 7502 2308 1

Printed and bound in Italy by G. Canale & CSpA, Turin

Acknowledgements
The author would like to thank the following for their advice and support: Steve Knight, Nikki van der Gaag, Chris Mason, Esther Gill, Trevor Jones and John Palmer.

Picture acknowledgements
Carousel 40 (Charlotte McPherson), 41 (Louise Davies); Howard Davies 15, 22, 23, 45, 47, 50, 51, 58; IFAW 18 (Thomas Grimm); Impact Photos Ltd 4 (Gavin Goulder), 9 (Tom Webster), 12 (Piers Cavendish), 14 (Sally Fear), 21 (Jorn St Jerneklar), 24 (Caroline Penn), 25 (Caroline Penn), 26 (Peter Whyte), 27, 33 (Stewart Weir), 46 (Crispin Hughes), 48, 57 (Chris Moyse); Mary Evans Picture Library 6, 8, 10; Panos Pictures 17 (Caroline Penn), 19 (Peter Barker), 39 (Maria Luiza Carvalho), 44, 52 (Neil Cooper), 54 (Sean Sprague), 55 (Sean Sprague), 59; Photri Inc 16 (Jeff Greenberg); Popperfoto 5, 7, 11 (Yun Suk-bong), 13 (Shamil Zhumatov), 20 (Nikhil Bhattacharya), 28 (Mark Baker), 30 (Charles Platiau), 31 (Fred Prouser), 32 (Sergei Karpukhin), 34 (Kieran Doherty), 35, 36 (Mike Hutchings), 37 (Jose Manuel Ribeiro), 38 (Robert Giroux), 42, 49 (Glab Garanich); RNIB 53.

Cover photograph by Howard Davies.

Contents

What is a charity?

At some time or other we have all helped someone who is in need. We may have spent time with a friend who needed a shoulder to cry on, gone shopping for an elderly neighbour, or given money to a homeless person in the street. These are all 'acts of charity'.

Throughout history people have helped others less well off than themselves. In ancient societies, such as those of Greece and Rome, provision was made to help the poor and disadvantaged. In Europe, in the Middle Ages, collections were made in churches to support almshouses, hospitals and orphanages for the poor.

The work of charities takes many forms. Here a young Albanian girl receives a toy from an aid convoy.

All the world's major religions, including Islam, Judaism, Christianity and Buddhism, recognize the importance of encouraging people to help others.

Giving as a part of everyday life

Muslims consider it a duty to pay *zakat*. Originally this was a tax levied on wealthy members of the community to help the poor. Only when this was paid was the person considered to be pure and good. *Zakat* is no longer collected by the state but giving to charity and the poor is still an important part of Muslim life.

These needy Palestinians are receiving food from a soup kitchen funded by wealthy Arab families.

Charities as institutions

Charities, also known today as 'non-profit' and 'voluntary' organizations, formalize acts of kindness and generosity. They bring together people who want to help others and raise money to enable their activities to take place.

Many charities start when small groups of people get together and decide that 'something has to be done'. These charities are often small and remain operating at a community level.

Other charities employ hundreds, sometimes thousands, of people and have massive financial turnovers. Many of the people who work for charities do so voluntarily – they are not paid. Large charities, as well as having thousands of volunteers, also employ paid staff.

The work charities do may take many different forms and be for many different causes. A charity could be a university, a theatre, a home for lost cats, a group of people encouraging others to recycle their waste, or a development agency working in countries all over the world.

Talking point

'The world has enough for everyone's need but not for everyone's greed.'

Mahatma Gandhi (1869–1948), Indian civil rights leader

What do you think Gandhi meant when he said this? What role do you think charities have in making sure everyone's needs are met?

The origins of charities

In Britain, charities as formal organizations first appeared in the nineteenth century. This was a time when the Industrial Revolution had led to mixed fortunes for the population. For some it had created enormous wealth but for others, forced to leave the countryside to seek work in the towns and cities, it had led to destitution and terrible poverty. There were very few measures in place to help those who fell on bad times. If someone lost their job or was too ill to work they were put in the poor house and virtually abandoned.

In the nineteenth century many middle-class women were moved by the plight of the poor and visited them in their homes, offering comfort, food and clothing.

A new home in Canada

The St Patrick's Society of Montreal was founded in 1834. The Society helped thousands of victims of the great Irish famine of 1846 when they arrived in Canada as refugees.

Many people were horrified by what was going on and decided to do something to help. It became quite fashionable for middle-class people, especially women, to volunteer their services in various charitable ways. The idea of the 'bountiful lady' was common across Europe, Canada and the USA by the end of the nineteenth century.

Angela Burdett-Coutts (1814–1906) lived in nineteenth-century London, and was the heir to a huge family fortune. She set up many projects to help the poor, such as providing food and cheap housing. She also had schools built so that poor children could have an education, and there is still a school in London named after her. She was involved in setting up the National Society for the Prevention of Cruelty to Children (NSPCC) and the Royal Society for the Prevention of Cruelty to Animals (RSPCA). These have grown into major charities in Britain today.

Baroness Burdett-Coutts did a huge amount to 'institutionalize' charity in the nineteenth century by setting up schools and providing cheap housing for the homeless.

Case study

In 1859, during the War of Italian Unification, Jean-Henry Dunant (1828–1910) was travelling in northern Italy. He arrived in the village of Castiglione on the evening following a battle. Nine thousand wounded soldiers had taken refuge in the church.

For several days and nights, Dunant worked alongside local women to help the wounded by washing and dressing their wounds and handing out tobacco, tea and fruit.

The experience gave Dunant the idea to form relief societies to take care of wounded people in wartime. He also came up with the idea of having an international agreement between all countries, so that prisoners of war would be well looked after. This was the basis for the Geneva Convention and the origin of the Red Cross.

Jean-Henry Dunant, Swiss founder of the Red Cross, pictured in 1901 when he received the Nobel Peace Prize.

In 1901 Dunant received the Nobel Peace Prize. Today the International Committee of the Red Cross is one of the largest and best-known humanitarian charities in the world. It has extended its peacetime work to giving medical aid and help to people afflicted by major disasters such as earthquakes, floods and famines.

Branches of the Red Cross now exist in many countries of the world, helping the victims of war and providing shelter for refugees. The American Red Cross, for example, assists in more than 50,000 disaster relief efforts annually, ranging from family house fires to major disasters.

Today the International Red Cross operates all over the world, providing food and medical help to disaster victims.

One of the best-known philanthropists in the USA was Andrew Carnegie (1835–1919), who devoted the latter part of his life to giving away most of the huge fortune he had made in the steel industry. Although he did not have a formal education himself he was very interested in books and he helped to set up nearly 1,700 libraries in the USA and Britain. He believed that it was his duty to return to society some of the vast fortune he considered he had been lucky enough to amass.

The industrial depressions in western Europe during the 1920s and 1930s plunged many into extreme poverty. The need for charities was again highlighted as free milk and food parcels for children were supplied. The First and Second World Wars also saw the origins of many international development charities, such as Oxfam and Save the Children.

A cartoon of Andrew Carnegie from the magazine *Punch*, 29 May 1901. Among his many other acts of generosity, Carnegie donated £2 million towards the establishment of free education at the four Scottish universities of the time: Edinburgh, Glasgow, St Andrew's and Aberdeen.

Types of charity

Charities are active all over the world and in every area of human life. They make a huge contribution to society. People are sometimes motivated to start charities for religious reasons – to do 'good works' and to spread a religious message – and sometimes simply out of general humanitarian concerns. In many countries there are financial benefits to being a charity, in terms of tax concessions.

A member of the Salvation Army collecting for the poor in Seoul, South Korea. The Salvation Army combines charitable works with a religious message, and operates all over the world.

Charity law

Because of these tax concessions, and also to safeguard the money the public donates, there are many laws and regulations relating to charities.

Laws dictate which organizations can become charities, and determine what they can and cannot do. These laws vary considerably from country to country.

In England and Wales, laws are particularly strict. The activities of charities are overseen by a government body, the Charity Commission. Some organizations, which are registered as charities elsewhere in the world, are not allowed to be charities in England and Wales. One example is Amnesty International, an organization that campaigns for human rights, which is not recognized as a charity because it is considered to have a 'political' purpose.

Much English and Welsh charity law is based on an Act of Parliament dating back to 1601, which states that charities should be for the relief of poverty, the benefit of the community, the advancement of religion or the advancement of education.

Some people feel charity laws are too complicated and out of date. Even those working for charities are not always clear about what they can or cannot do. For example, the Moonies, a highly controversial religious organization, and Eton College, an expensive, prestigious English school, are both registered charities, but the environmental group Greenpeace is not. This is not to say that the Moonies and Eton should not be charities, or that Greenpeace should be, but many people do not understand why some organizations are charities and others are not.

> ### Talking point
>
> 'Once it [charity] was a way for the rich to pay for the education of the poor. Now it's a way for the poor taxpayer to pay for the education of Prince William at Eton.'
>
> Polly Toynbee, journalist,
> *Guardian*, 4 May 1998
>
> Eton College charges a fee of £12,000 per year, and the sons of Britain's most prestigious families go there. And yet, because it is a charity, Eton benefits from tax concessions. Do you think this is fair?

Students at the exclusive Eton College – a registered charity.

In the USA, charities have to register with the local tax department, which oversees the way in which they conduct their affairs financially. Otherwise charities are accountable to the public. If they are seen to be a good charity people will support them with their donations. There is less reliance on the government to keep an eye on charities in the USA than there is in England and Wales.

In the USA charities need to be able to show that their income derives from many different sources; it cannot come from just one or a few benefactors. This makes charities more secure as they do not become reliant on one source of funding for their income.

What do charities do?

The range of work covered by charities is vast. Some focus on specific groups of people, for example children, senior citizens, people with disabilities, people with particular illnesses, ex-criminals and – by far the largest group of all – the poor.

A woman threshes wheat in the ruins of her home in the village of Ghanji in northern Afghanistan after an earthquake in February 1998. Aid agencies had considerable difficulty reaching this remote area, but humanitarian aid was eventually delivered, helping to save many lives.

Charities also focus on specific areas, such as the environment, animal welfare and racial harmony. Some charities help to save thousands of lives every year, particularly after disasters and emergencies such as earthquakes, famines and floods.

Traditionally we often think of charities as handing out food and blankets. In fact they provide a much wider range of services, such as giving advice and support, mounting campaigns, funding building projects and writing books to increase people's awareness of their cause.

Working with animals

You probably know about guide dogs which help blind and partially-sighted people. Dogs also help people who are deaf, by being trained to alert them when the doorbell rings or if an alarm goes off. Dogs can also help people who are wheelchair users by fetching items for them, and even helping with the shopping.

In Boston, Massachusetts, there is a non-profit organization called Helping Hands which trains capuchin monkeys to help quadriplegics – people who do not have the use of either their arms or legs. The monkeys perform simple, everyday tasks like fetching food or a drink, picking up a dropped item, turning lights on or off and even putting on music.

A guide dog, supplied and trained by a charity, helps its owner to cross the road safely.

The relief of poverty

The biggest group of charities are those tackling poverty. Poverty is worldwide. It is present in the richer countries of the West, in the USA and Europe, as well as in the developing countries of Africa, Asia and South America.

Charities working in developing countries are also known as 'voluntary aid agencies' or 'non-governmental organizations'. There are literally thousands of voluntary aid agencies, but some of the largest, like Oxfam and Save the Children in the UK, CARE Incorporated and Project Hope in the USA, and Médecins Sans Frontières (MSF) in France, are household names. Typically they respond to emergencies in developing countries. The main part of their work, though, is with local groups, helping people help themselves to improve the quality of their lives. This is sometimes called 'community development'.

In addition to the large agencies, there are many small charities started by people after they have visited a particular place. Often towns and communities in the West have a link with communities in developing countries. They set up charities to channel funds to these places, which help with community development.

'Community development' takes many forms but is often concerned with helping people provide themselves with clean water in order to avoid diseases like typhoid and dysentery.

A two-way relationship

The charity One Heart raises money for the people of Cameroon by selling CDs by the band Baka Beyond, whose music is based on the traditional songs of Cameroon.

15

Within the USA and Europe, charities who work with the poor in their own countries have adopted this idea of community development. The feeling is that it is not enough to 'hand out' food, blankets and clothing but that an approach is needed which empowers people to make their own decisions about their own lives.

Despite these efforts there are so many people in the world who live in some degree of poverty that it is very difficult for charities to decide who they should support. Not everyone in need can be helped and difficult choices sometimes have to be made.

Environmental and animal welfare organizations

Environmental and animal welfare organizations are concerned about the way in which our consumer society damages the world around it. They work at every level from the local (conserving a meadow of rare wild flowers for example) to the global (for example, supporting agreements between governments to cut industrial pollution). Much of their work is centred on educating the public about what is causing damage to the environment and how this damage can be prevented.

Charities in England and Wales

There are 187,000 charities registered with the Charity Commission. In 1997 the total annual income of all registered charities in England and Wales was £18.3 billion. The top five charities by voluntary donations in 1995 were:

Church Commissioners	£107.1 million
National Trust	£ 53.5 million
Save the Children	£ 34.1 million
Oxfam	£ 33.4 million
Barnado's	£ 30.3 million

Source: Charity Commission

A shelter for the homeless in the USA. Is it enough for charities to 'hand out' food and blankets to those in need?

Although money is important to support the work these charities do, informing people about their cause is often more important. Animal welfare groups encourage their members and supporters to campaign and demonstrate against animals being used to test cosmetics, or against fox hunting or seal culling. These charities face dilemmas when their causes come into conflict with what may be called 'human welfare' – when testing on animals is for medical research, or when the hunting of animals is a people's only source of food or is essential to their livelihood. A good example is the Inuit people of Canada and Greenland who hunt whales and seals for food.

In the UK, the RSPCA is allowed to campaign and demonstrate against animal testing for products such as cosmetics, but they cannot demonstrate when the animal testing is for medical research. In this case it is the UK government that is deciding what a charity should or should not do. Some people feel this is wrong, and that the RSPCA suffers unfairly because members of the public who disagree with animal testing for medical research may choose not to donate money to the charity.

Charities in the USA

There are more than 650,000 charities registered with the Internal Revenue Service in the USA. The top five charities by voluntary donations in 1996 were:

Salvation Army	$1 billion
American Red Cross	$479.9 million
American Cancer Society	$426.7 million
Emery University Atlanta	$415.4 million
Catholic Charities USA	$386.5 million

Source: *Chronicle of Philanthropy*

The Inuit return to camp after hunting whales for food.

Case study

The International Fund for Animal Welfare (IFAW) is an international organization with offices in countries all over the world including the USA, Canada, South Africa, Australia and the UK. Brian Davies, a Welsh-born Canadian, started the organization in 1969. He was horrified by the culling of seals on the ice floes off the east coast of Canada. Since then IFAW has expanded its activities, and its campaigns include elephants, bears, whales and seals.

Although it is registered as a charity everywhere else in the world, in England and Wales only the educational side of IFAW's work is deemed as charitable. Therefore a separate organization has been set up, the IFAW Charitable Trust, which produces information and resources for schools. The rest of the organization in England and Wales is not registered as a charity.

The *Song of the Whale* is the IFAW yacht, which travels the world's oceans studying whales, dolphins, turtles and other marine life.

Medical research charities

Medical research and health-related charities attract large amounts of funding from the public and from governments. In Canada, health-related charities receive 56 per cent of their funding from the government. In the UK, £340 million was contributed by charities to medical research in the year 1995–6.

Doctors and scientists around the world are trying to find cures for conditions such as cancer and heart disease. As these are major killers, particularly in the West, this would clearly be of benefit to everyone. Charities conducting this kind of research receive a large income from the public, partly because so many people have had friends or relations who have been affected by these diseases.

Money well spent?
The cost of a protective suit designed for use during chemical warfare would pay for a micro-centrifuge for DNA analysis, crucial in research undertaken by cancer charities.

Research also includes the study of tropical diseases. These include malaria, which kills thousands of people each year, especially in developing countries. Other diseases for which there is currently no cure – such as the muscle-wasting motor neurone disease and AIDS – have charities specifically to support those suffering from the disease and to encourage and fund research into a cure.

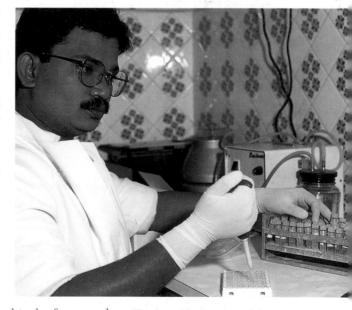

Most medical charities doing this kind of research are based in universities or at specialized laboratories, and their income is supplemented by government grants.

Much medical research is funded by charities.

Religious organizations

A certain number of charities are run by religious organizations. They operate in just about every sphere of humanitarian work, from helping people with disabilities to supporting overseas development projects. In some cases this work stems from many years ago when missionaries travelled the world to convert people to Christianity. This remains an important part of some religious charities' work, but nowadays most say they are not interested in converting people, they just want to help.

The 'saint of the gutters'

Mother Teresa was famous throughout the world for her work with the poor of Calcutta in India. She was known as the 'saint of the gutters'. In 1949 she created the Missionaries of Charity, an order of nuns. She saw their work as a religious calling above all else. She said: 'We are first of all religious; we are not social workers, not teachers, not nurses or doctors, we are religious sisters. We serve Jesus in the poor.' In 1979 she received the Nobel Peace Prize.

However, her work received criticism. People accused her of putting preaching to the poor above relieving their suffering, and of telling them that they must 'accept their fate'. Others rose to her defence, saying that she was truly holy and the work her nuns were doing was of immense value to those who benefited from it.

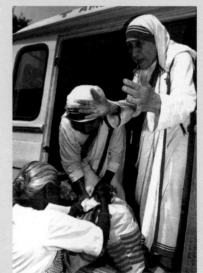

Mother Teresa died in 1997, aged 87.

Mother Teresa of Calcutta welcoming a mentally ill woman into her care.

Who benefits from charities?

You do not have to be poor to benefit from a charity. In fact we probably all benefit from the work of charities at some point in our lives, although we might never be aware of it. At one extreme our life may be saved by some medical treatment developed by the work of a charity; at the other we may, as children, have played in a playground equipped by a local charity. We never know when we might need the services of a charity, and some people see giving to charity as a good investment for their own future.

Talking point

'Why should the poor be grateful for the crumbs that fall from the rich man's table? They should be seated at the meal.'

Oscar Wilde, Irish writer and dramatist, 1854–1900

Do you think people should be grateful for charity, or should charity be a 'right'?

Victims of famine as a result of war in Somalia. Such scenes are commonly associated with the work of charities. However, many people are not aware that providing immediate famine relief is only a small part of the work carried out by charities like Save the Children and Project Hope.

However, the image that most people probably have when they think of those who benefit from charity is that of the victims of disasters or war, somewhere in the developing world. These people may be in need as a result of drought. They may have been forced to flee from their homes because of conflict. They may instead be the victims of a natural disaster such as an earthquake or a hurricane.

In order to operate efficiently, charities need to employ skilled professionals, such as this doctor who works for the charity Merlin.

We do not, however, hear a lot about the everyday work of charities and those who benefit. Once the emergency is over and no longer on our television screens, the aid agencies continue to work, training people to become farmers or helping them learn to read and write. As a result, people benefit in a sustainable way over a long period of time.

Charity workers

Obviously the people who benefit from charities are those for whom the charities are set up in the first place. But others benefit too.

Charities employ thousands of people who do an enormous range of jobs. They include vets, nurses, teachers, aid workers, accountants, fundraisers, retail specialists, doctors, office cleaners and telephonists. There are even special employment agencies for people who want to work for a charity.

Most charities find that they have little difficulty filling vacant posts. People are very attracted to the idea of working for a charity, because they feel they will be doing something to contribute to the welfare of others through their work.

In some cases the people at the top of charitable organizations may be on quite high salaries, although they are usually paid less than they would receive for a similar job in the commercial world. However, according to the Internal Revenue Service, the heads of the largest charities in the USA received large pay rises in 1997.

Essential volunteers

In Canada, nearly 40 per cent of charities have no full-time paid staff, and 21 per cent have only one full-time paid employee. It would be impossible for these charities to continue to exist without voluntary help.

A volunteer for the Refugee Council helps an asylum seeker with his application.

They are among the top 1 per cent of wage earners in the USA. The argument in favour of such high salaries is that unless charities are prepared to pay their directors similar amounts to those working in commerce, they will be unable to recruit people with the right skills and experience needed for the job.

Volunteers

Not everyone who works for a charity is paid. Many people work for nothing and get a lot of satisfaction from doing so. They work in the offices and the second-hand shops of their chosen charity, and spend much of their own time supporting its campaigns. People can get a lot of satisfaction from helping in this way, but it also has social benefits, providing an opportunity to meet like-minded people.

Organizations like the Peace Corps in the USA, and Voluntary Service Overseas (VSO) in Britain, send young people all over the world to work for one or two years as teachers, nurses or doctors, or on agricultural and scientific projects. They gain valuable experience which can stand them in good stead for getting a job later on.

People also volunteer their services to organizations like the Samaritans, who provide confidential emotional support to anyone who is depressed or thinking about committing suicide. Volunteers are carefully trained to be skilled listeners and provide a valuable service to the community.

Case study

VSO is an organization that sends skilled men and women to work with local people in 61 different developing countries all over the world. Since it began in 1958, VSO has sent 23,000 volunteers to work overseas. Volunteers usually go abroad for two years. Their air fares and accommodation are paid, and they receive a small allowance which is in line with the pay-rates of local people in the country they are visiting.

A VSO volunteer demonstrates new agricultural techniques at a college in Thailand.

To qualify as a VSO volunteer you must be between 20 and 70 years old, have a formal qualification and some work experience. Volunteers are selected very carefully, and many more people apply than are accepted.

Particularly in demand are health professionals, builders, carpenters and textile designers. Volunteers pass on their skills to the community where they work, so that when they leave, the work they have begun can continue without them. When volunteers return home they often join a local VSO group which enables them to share their experiences with others who have returned from different countries. VSO also helps ex-volunteers in their search for employment once home, and VSO experience is highly valued by a large number of employers.

Nick applied to VSO when he was 23. He was sent to Papua New Guinea and worked as a medical assistant in a hospital. After a year and a half he returned home and went on to qualify as a doctor.

Nick's experience with VSO helped him to understand some of the differences between working in the health service in the West and in a developing country. As a direct result of his experience with VSO he later worked in the field of tuberculosis control in east Nepal, and then as a nutritionist for a large development agency in Cambodia. He now works in England.

Nick says: 'My overseas experience as a volunteer made me look at the world in a more global way. I want to help others to share in the kind of invaluable experiences I have had, particularly young people.'

A VSO medical assistant in Tanzania.

Feeling good

The fact that charities exist can also be seen to benefit society as a whole. Giving to charity can make us feel good and charities make it easy for us to do this. Some people find that being kind makes them feel better about themselves, and that it improves their reputation and causes others to respect them more.

If we trust the charity we can be confident that the money we give will be used well. However, this can also make us a bit lazy when it comes to helping others in a direct way. We think we have done our bit and we do not need to do anything else. Perhaps there are other ways in which we could make a contribution, such as volunteering to help out in some way in the local community, for example at a day centre or a school.

Raising funds

In order to do their work, charities have constantly to find money. There is increasing competition between all the charities for the comparatively small amount of money people are prepared to give. As the number of charities grows, so the competition for funds increases.

Where does the money come from?

Not all the money charities receive comes from the public. Funds are given in the form of government grants, donations from big businesses, and trust funds. National and local governments give grants, especially where the charity is undertaking work which is part of the government's responsibility. For some charities by far and away the largest proportion of their income comes from these grants, and this is of increasing importance to them. But most, especially small charities, rely on the 'voluntary contributions' which bring in money from the public.

Going out with a collecting tin is still one of the most common methods of fundraising.

Traditional methods

The most traditional forms of fundraising are street-to-street collections or the rattling of a tin on a street corner. The idea of the 'charity shop', where people donate used clothes or bric-à-brac for the shop to sell, has also been around for many years and has been very successful.

There are many stories of people leaving millions in their will to the local cats' home, but legacies do provide a very important source of income for many charities. For some charities 60 per cent of their income is from wills.

Giving to charity

- In Britain the combined charities have an income of some £17 billion a year, of which about £5 billion is donated. The National Lottery has added another £300 million a year to that income.
- In 1996, people in the USA gave $150.7 billion to charity.

Charities take legacies very seriously. They employ experts to advise those people thinking of leaving money to them on how they should make out their will. When someone dies from an illness such as cancer, the relations often ask people to donate to a charity researching cures for the illness, rather than buying flowers for the funeral.

People enjoy combining raising money with a specific activity. They ask people to sponsor them to achieve a goal. Sometimes this is related to the cause they are collecting for, like going without food for 24 hours to raise money for famine victims, or is an activity that requires some commitment or stamina, such as running a marathon, or swimming a mile.

Armchair fundraising

Today, we do not need to walk past the person standing on the street corner with a collecting tin to be asked to give money to charity. Fundraisers have found ways of reaching us in our homes.

'Cold mailing' is when thousands of people are written to at the same time, often as part of a specific appeal. They may be people who have previously had nothing whatsoever to do with the charity. The names are purchased as a computer database.

People often take part in sponsored events to raise money for charity. In Sydney, Australia, the 'Rat Race' takes place every year, in which office workers run a three-kilometre race through the city to raise money for the Red Cross.

Although many people regard such requests as simply junk mail and put them straight in the bin, many others respond. Charities usually find cold mailing an effective way to fundraise, even though there is a fairly high initial outlay.

As part of a mailing some charities send a 'free' gift, such as a pen, greetings cards, or even a coin. This is intended to encourage the recipient to 'pay' for the gift and to add a donation of their own. This puts quite a lot of pressure on people to donate. They do not, of course, have to, and people often throw the 'free' gift away.

A comparatively new method of fundraising is 'telemarketing'. This is a bit like cold mailing but involves telephoning people in their homes. People are asked either to donate money to a particular cause, or to take part in a fundraising activity such as a street collection. Charities achieve quite a good response from this method of fundraising, and it can be used to keep those who already support the charity in touch with its activities. However, many people feel such telephone calls are an intrusion.

At the end of a hard day

'I had a terrible day in the office, my train was late, I'd just sat down to have my dinner when someone phoned me from some charity asking me to send them a donation. I think this is an invasion of my privacy and I told them so.'

Steve Knight, information technology consultant

Another way to reach millions of people is through 'telethons'. In recent years, these have become very popular in many countries including the USA, Canada, Britain, France and Spain.

The annual French Telethon raised millions of pounds in 1997 for research into genetic diseases in children. The Telethon goes out live on French television for 30 hours.

A telethon is a television programme, lasting anything up to 24 hours or more, where viewers pledge donations by phoning the television station. They stand a chance of having their name read out on the programme. Stars and celebrities appear and favourite television clips are shown. Local community groups organize sponsored events which are featured on the programme, giving them good publicity. Increasingly, an important part of the telethon is giving people information in the form of short films and interviews about the causes for which money is being collected.

Why people give more

It is generally accepted that some causes are much easier to raise funds for than others. Anything to do with babies or young children is popular, and people are usually moved by television pictures and newspaper reports of people in disaster situations. Following the death of Diana, Princess of Wales, in 1997, money flooded into the memorial fund set up to benefit her favourite charities.

But other causes, such as rehabilitation programmes for criminals or drug abusers, are more difficult to raise funds for. AIDS charities were very unpopular until many film stars and celebrities (in particular, Diana, Princess of Wales) gave their support. Celebrities can give an enormous boost to a charity. Some get very involved in the work of the charity, while others are no more than figureheads.

The marathon telethon
The largest telethon in the USA is produced by the Children's Miracle Network and takes place in June each year. It is on air for 21 hours and raises money for more than 160 children's hospitals in North America. It is broadcast on 200 stations and reaches over 100 million households.

Billy Crystal, Whoopi Goldberg and Robin Williams help to raise money for the homeless in the USA by hosting 'Comic Relief VII'.

Case study

'I don't have all the answers. But I know what questions to ask. And, after all, I can't take it with me.'

George Soros

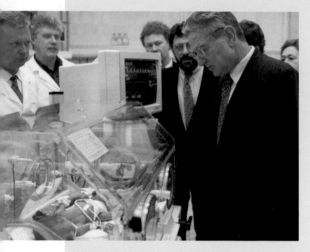

George Soros visiting the Moscow Medical Academy in 1997.

George Soros is an international financier and one of the richest people in the world. Some would say that he is also one of the most generous. In 1994 he gave 14 per cent of his income to good causes.

George Soros was born in Hungary in 1932. He became a millionaire by anticipating changes in the economies of countries all over the world. Perhaps because of his own personal struggles and experiences of poverty in his youth, he has given enormous amounts of money to charities over the years. In some cases the money he has donated to support charity projects in developing countries has exceeded the total amount of aid given by the US government.

In 1992 Soros gave $50 million to agencies working in Bosnia. He gave another $50 million to the Emma Lazarus Fund, a project set up to help legal immigrants settle when they first arrive in the USA, and $12 million to the Algebra Project, which helps children to improve their mathematical skills.

Although he has given away millions of dollars, George Soros is still an exceptionally wealthy man. Some people would argue that generosity may be better measured not only by the percentage of income donated but also by the level of sacrifice this entails. However, there is no denying that George Soros's donations to charities have helped thousands of people, and probably saved many lives.

Why people give less

The amount of money people are giving to charities is falling. This may be due to people's concern about whether their money is going to the right place. It only takes one piece of bad publicity about how a charity is spending its donations to cause concern about the way all charities are spending their funds.

Other reasons suggested for the fall in charitable donations include unemployment and the influence of lotteries. For most people, giving to charity is not a priority. If they become unemployed, then making no donations is a way of saving money. The establishment of lotteries in many countries has meant that people spend money on lottery tickets rather than donating direct to charities. Many charities, though, do benefit from lottery grants.

Lotteries

Governments in many countries have set up lotteries designed to raise funds for 'good works'. Many charities receive funding from governments in the form of lottery grants, which help to make them more financially secure. However, it is the lottery boards who decide which charities will benefit, not the people who buy the lottery tickets.

In the UK, charities have to apply for a lottery grant in order to be considered. The application process can be complex, and often requires expertise to succeed. As a result, charities which are skilled in making applications have more chance of success.

The UK National Lottery has resulted in large grants for some charities but a drop in donations for others.

Charities that fail in their application for grants, or that do not apply at all, can suffer a fall in donations, because people may choose to spend their money on a lottery ticket rather than giving to charity.

Company funding

A very important source of income for charities comes from large companies and big business. As well as recognizing that they have a moral obligation to support charities, there are tax advantages and it is good publicity for large firms to be seen to support charities.

It is the responsibility of charities to do their best for their beneficiaries, which means raising as much money as possible. But should they take money from anyone who offers it to them?

Company interests

In some cases it may be very much in a company's interests to be associated with a particular charity. The association may provide them with good publicity and advertising. For example, a manufacturer of powdered milk for babies may feel that if they support a charity which promotes natural childbirth then the public will associate them with something that is natural and good.

The dollar hamburger

On Wednesday 6 May 1998 a dollar from every Big Mac sold at McDonald's restaurants across Canada went to a variety of local children's charities.

Charities must do their best for their beneficiaries, such as this homeless man receiving food and drink at Christmas supplied by a charity in New York. But should charities accept donations regardless of the donor?

But what if the business of the company offering the money is at direct odds with the work of the charity? For example, a cigarette manufacturer may wish to donate money to a cancer charity.

Accepting money in such controversial circumstances can be counter-productive for the charity. Existing supporters may be upset and withdraw their support and funding.

Talking point

'It is actually very difficult for registered charities to refuse voluntary donations.'
Director of the Institute of Charity Fundraising Managers

How should charities decide which donations to accept and which to reject?

Collecting for a cancer charity. This supporter might be less willing to give up his time to the charity if it was accepting money from a cigarette manufacturer.

Raising awareness

Most charities spend a proportion of their income on campaigning and education. Why do they do this, rather than spend all the money they raise directly on the causes for which people gave the money?

Most charities seem to have three types of supporter. The largest group is made up of people who contribute money on a regular basis but are not particularly interested in a deeper involvement. A second group contributes regularly and is interested

in 'knowing more' about the charity's work. Finally, the third group wants not only to 'know more' but to 'do more' and become involved in some kind of action to support the charity and its causes.

Charities need to encourage the first group, as it is an important source of funding. They also need to respond to the needs of their supporters in the two other groups who want to get more involved. This means informing them about the work the charity does and about the issues that motivate it.

This cyclist is competing in a sponsored cycle race to raise money for a charity that is trying to save the endangered white rhino.

Helping people to know and do more

Helping the public – and in particular a charity's supporters – to understand some of the issues behind the scenes can often be the best way of improving the quality of people's lives and furthering the charity's cause.

At an international level, development agencies campaign to change policies that they believe make life more difficult for the people with whom they work.

For example, some agencies campaign against the manufacture and export of landmines, which kill and maim 2,000 people a month, many of them children. They publish leaflets giving statistics about the number of people killed and maimed. They issue press releases and try to get television coverage. Once people are aware of the situation, the charities believe, they will put pressure on politicians to stop producing and exporting landmines.

The visit by Diana, Princess of Wales, to Angola in 1997 raised the public's awareness about landmines.

Other agencies encourage their supporters to lobby for more government money to be spent on aid programmes – governments spend far more on aid than charities could ever spend – and to insist that it is spent on projects that will actually benefit the poor. Some agencies lobby governments and financial institutions in the West to cancel the debts of developing countries so that these countries can spend more on helping their own poor.

Often, a charity finds that raising public awareness and affecting how people behave is one of the best ways to help those who are in need. For example, children who have eczema are often bullied at school because of their appearance. If children are made aware of what eczema really is, and how unpleasant it can be, bullying can be replaced by understanding. Charities work to raise awareness about conditions like eczema, asthma and epilepsy by providing resources to schools, such as information packs, and working closely with teachers.

Taking action

Charities use a number of methods to highlight their causes. They organize marches and demonstrations, collect signatures on petitions or organize letter-writing campaigns to politicians.

Marching for awareness

In July 1997, the annual march for AIDS in San Francisco raised more than $3.5 million. One of the aims of the march was to raise awareness of AIDS among the public, and it was attended by 25,000 people.

The AIDS memorial quilt in Washington, USA, October 1996. The quilt contained more than 37,000 panels, each dedicated to someone who had died of AIDS, and was displayed as part of a weekend of activities aimed at raising people's awareness of the disease.

If politicians can see that there is strong support for a particular charity's cause, they are more likely to adopt its policies.

Charities sometimes encourage people to do certain things that they believe will help their cause. Buying goods in the shops, like coffee and tea, that are 'fairly traded' means that the people growing the product, who are usually quite poor, get a higher percentage of the price paid for it. Environmental charities encourage people to buy goods that have been produced without harming the environment or that have not been tested on animals.

However, charities are not pressure groups and they have to be careful not to appear so. At all times they must be able to show that their campaigning is based on their own direct experience. The action they take must be appropriate and must not undermine the reputation, and consequently the effectiveness, of the charity. And, of course, what they do must be legal.

'Fair trade' agreements, often instigated by charities, mean that people who grow products like coffee beans receive a fair price for their goods and are not exploited.

Case study

A Carousel music workshop.

Carousel is a small arts charity that works with people with learning difficulties. It provides opportunities for people to take part in a wide range of different activities that encourage them to be creative and use their imaginations. The activities supported by Carousel include music-making, dance and art.

For example, Carousel co-ordinates a dance company called High Spin. Each member helps to develop the dance and the music. The end result is performed at arts festivals and theatres. The performances are of high quality and audiences are impressed by the energy and commitment shown by all involved.

This work is important as it provides opportunities for people with learning difficulties to prove to themselves what they can do. For them it can be very empowering, and it helps them to find ways in which they can express themselves. However it is also vitally important because it helps the public to understand that people with learning difficulties can do all kinds of things. Presenting themselves in this positive way helps other people to understand them, and the work of Carousel, far better. Raising awareness is one of the most important aspects of Carousel's work.

'Carousel shows us all a world where difference is a source of creativity and expression, a world where individuality is expressed in pursuit of common goals and a world where everyone's ability is prized. That's a world anyone would want to be part of.'

Simon Fanshawe, broadcaster and writer

Members of Carousel perform at a street festival.

Getting political?

There is always the danger when presenting controversial issues to the public that some will accuse charities of being biased or even political. In England and Wales, guidelines produced by the Charity Commission say that it is wrong for charities 'inappropriately to seek to influence government policy, local or central, home or abroad, or to advocate changes in the law or the retention of existing laws'. The Commission also says that political publicity in the guise of education is not charitable. However, it is not easy for anyone to say what is 'inappropriate' and what is 'political' – it is a very grey area.

Campaigning by charities to raise awareness, mobilize public opinion and influence government policy can arouse strong feelings. On the one hand, many people think that charities should be allowed to campaign freely to change public policy on any issue if it is relevant to their work and if they have direct experience to offer. On the other hand, some argue that such campaigning is a misuse of charity funds, a misdirection of effort by charities and a misuse of the tax concessions from which charities benefit.

Although the environmental group Greenpeace relies on voluntary staffing and funding it is not registered as a charity because of its policy of 'direct, non-violent action', such as this demonstration against the nuclear tests carried out by Pakistan in 1998.

Talking point

'When I give food to the hungry they call me a saint; when I ask why the poor are hungry they call me a communist.'

Dom Hélder Câmara, former archbishop of Recife, Brazil

Charities have sometimes got into trouble for their campaigning work when people have accused them of being 'political'. Do you think charities should be involved in campaigning work?

Where does the money go?

The public can sometimes seem to be more concerned about where the money they donate to charity goes than they are about where their taxes go! They can be quick to judge charities for wasting money, but is this really the case?

Accountability

All charities are required to produce annual accounts showing where the money people have given them each year has gone. These accounts are available to the public and show how much has been spent on administration, how much on fundraising and how much on actual charitable work. The accounts also show how much income the charity has had and where that money has come from.

Sometimes criticism has been directed at charities for spending money on administration. It is seen as money that is wasted. However, at the same time people also want to be reassured that their money is being spent wisely. These two things are not entirely compatible. The more people want to know about charities' spending, the more charities have to spend on administration to produce information leaflets and set up enquiry hot lines.

An example of annual spending by a charity. These figures come from Oxfam.

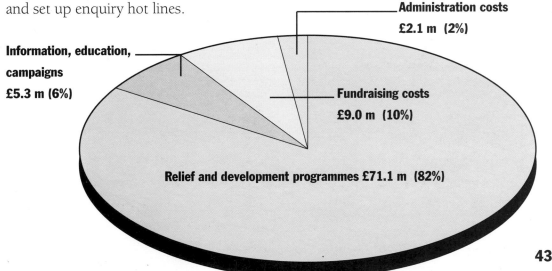

Administration costs
£2.1 m (2%)

Information, education, campaigns
£5.3 m (6%)

Fundraising costs
£9.0 m (10%)

Relief and development programmes £71.1 m (82%)

Even if charities are entirely run by volunteers, who receive no wages for the work they do, there are still expenses such as telephones, rent and stationery. It would be impossible for a charity to spend every single donation it received on its beneficiaries and none at all on administration.

Staff meet to discuss how their charity should be run.

Well run?

The vast majority of charities are well run and highly efficient. They have to be, if they are going to be successful and survive. It is rare for a charity to be set up in the first place with the intention of deceiving people out of their money and there are only a few cases of 'bogus' charities being exposed. Most fraud associated with charities is on a small scale and carried out by employees or volunteers. Fortunately such incidents are few and far between. However, when this does happen it usually attracts a great deal of bad publicity and can be very damaging for genuine charities.

A breach of trust

In 1998 two Oxfam charity shop workers were convicted of stealing goods from the shop, which should have been sold to raise money for the charity. A spokesperson for Oxfam said they had abused a position of trust, and that such incidents were extremely rare. Both workers were fined and required to do community service.

Case study

The war in Bosnia appeared nightly on our television screens. Two million people were left homeless and thousands were wounded, often by exploding landmines. It was estimated that over one million people suffered from post-traumatic stress disorders. Forty per cent of the country's health care system was destroyed.

As with so many disasters, people around the world responded to the powerful images they saw on television and in the newspapers by donating generously to aid agencies working in Bosnia. Some companies, however, made donations with little thought for the suffering of the people. They had their own image far more in mind.

At least half the drugs donated to aid agencies and the World Health Organization (WHO) during the war in Bosnia were found to be useless. Some companies donated drugs which were either well past their expiry dates or had labels that were illegible. Some donations included army medical supplies that were left over from the Second World War. Other drugs were

During the war in Bosnia, injured refugees needed medical help, but many donated drugs were useless.

totally inappropriate for the conditions in that part of the world – for example, treatments for leprosy, a disease not found in the former Yugoslavia. WHO and the aid agencies must now pay to dispose of the 17,000 tonnes of useless supplies with money that could have been spent far more usefully elsewhere.

The companies who made these donations were able to claim tax concessions for making charitable gifts, even though their contribution was not only useless but potentially dangerous.

In most countries there are bodies to oversee the functioning of charities, and guidelines are available to help people 'vet' a charity before donating to it. People can check the name of the charity to make sure that it is the right one and not one using a similar name. Donations can be made in the form of a cheque made out to the organization rather than in cash, and detailed information about the charity's work and finances can be asked for.

Talking point

'A place does exist in our society for charity, but at a local and direct level. My best advice is to avoid any organization that has a flash letterhead and logo, since one knows that a substantial amount of collected funds went into creating them and that a far larger amount probably goes towards the administrators' salaries.'

Anonymous letter to the *Guardian*, 7 May 1998

Do you agree with what this person is saying? If charity only happened at a local level what would happen to national medical research charities and international aid agencies? Is the way a charity presents itself important?

Stolen food aid being transported by camel. Even when donations are spent correctly, the food can end up in the wrong hands.

Does money go astray?

People are sometimes concerned that, having given their money, it doesn't go to the intended cause – to the people who need it. One concern is that money given to charities working in developing countries can end up in the hands of corrupt governments. However, it is not usually the case that overseas aid agencies work with governments; they work directly with local groups who help people in need.

Where does the money go?

On the other hand, governments do give aid directly to other governments, and this type of aid has frequently gone astray in the past. This type of corruption has been wrongly laid at the door of charities. It was not charity money that went astray but taxpayers' money. However, people still have every right to be angry about it.

Aid agencies try to work directly with groups who help poor people.

Get rich quick!

● The late President Mobutu Sese Seko of Zaïre once dismissed 7,000 teachers from Zaïrian schools on the grounds that there was not enough money to pay them. He owned 51 Mercedes Benz cars and lived in astonishing luxury on money that had come from Western aid.

● Ferdinand Marcos, president of the Philippines between 1965 and 1986, and his wife Imelda were estimated to have embezzled $10 billion, most of which came from foreign aid paid by Western taxpayers.

Behind the image

For most people the word 'charity' conjures up an image of helping others, kindness and 'good works'. But some associate 'charity' with images of pity and helplessness, and may even feel contempt towards those in need of help. People who receive charity can feel extremely uncomfortable and even angry about this.

Images of helplessness may generate income for charities, but do little for people's self-esteem.

Feeling good about charity

Imagine how you would feel if you needed help from a charity. Some people in such a situation feel as though it is an admission that they are not able to cope with their own life. They find the idea of being dependent on charity very demeaning. It can severely dent their pride. They resent the fact that other people see them as dependent or as victims.

Some people worry that charities only encourage people to become dependent on them. They argue that people come to expect a charity to help them out whenever they are in trouble, and that if charities did not exist people would try harder to help themselves and each other.

A necessary evil?

'I hate the whole idea of charity but I have to depend on it. So I'm grateful for it too.'

A single parent

The collapse of Communism has caused great hardship in Russia and forced many people to beg on the streets to survive. Being dependent on other people's charity can make you feel as if you can't cope with your own life, even if the situation is beyond your control.

However, people who receive some kind of help through charities are rarely completely helpless. Most are working hard to cope with their difficulties and to improve their situation. It is important to realize that we all need help at some time in our lives and we all benefit from charities either directly or indirectly. Some people are lucky enough not to have to use charity, or have friends and family who can help them. But it is a shame if this makes them feel that they are in any way superior.

People who receive charity are by no means completely helpless, and work to make the best use of the help that they receive.

Being involved

People who benefit from a charity frequently claim that they should have more say in how the charity is run. They have direct experience of the problem.

Therefore, they should be part of the solution. Involving people in this way is an important method of addressing the problem of people's self-esteem and feelings of worth.

An example of this is the way in which disabled people have accused some large charities of using outdated images of disability, which exaggerate the idea of dependence and try to make people feel sorry for the disabled, all in order to raise money. Disabled activists argue that charities should spend more time and money on the fight for civil rights legislation. They would also like to see more disabled people running charities for other disabled people.

Images and fundraising

No charity could exist without money. So before they do anything else they have to raise money. In order to do this they have to try to convince us, the general public, of the urgency of their cause.

We are bombarded by so many images all the time on our televisions and in the newspapers that charities will often try to shock us into realizing how serious their case is. They may even try to make us feel guilty. They know we haven't got much time so they try to get their message across simply and quickly. By doing this they sometimes give a false impression of what the situation is really like. In most cases it is quite complex and difficult to understand.

Powerful pictures

'Pictures have power. They can convey information and emotion. They can provoke a response and leave a lasting impression. The right pictures can mobilize people and change the course of events. It's a power that can be used for good or bad.'

Development agency leaflet

Few people could not be moved by this picture of Rwandan refugees being denied access to Zaïre. But to understand the situation properly, more information is needed than just a picture.

The stereotypical image of people in the developing world is that of someone with a begging bowl stretched out, imploring people for money or food. Not only is this often a false image but it also results in people developing very negative ideas about poor people as being passive and helpless. Charities have to take some responsibility for having promoted these kinds of images, even though this may have been unintentional.

Partly in response to what people who receive charity say and partly in response to a realization that they are conveying a false and damaging image, many charities have given a lot of thought to this problem. They have changed their logos and issued guidelines about the photographs that should be used and the language employed in fundraising advertisements.

Although many charities have changed their logos and the wording in their advertisements, some critics are still sceptical. They say that such changes are only for appearances and that they need to be more far-reaching.

Not just a starving dust bowl: ploughing in a fertile valley near Dessie in Ethiopia.

Talking point

'Of course we have more than our fair share of disasters. And of course we are grateful for the incredible generosity of people. But where is it shown how hard we work to solve our own problems? Where are the pictures of our rich culture, our ancient history, our beautiful countryside? Do they think Ethiopia is just one, big, starving dust bowl full of people waiting to die?'

Gebre Dori, Addis Ababa, Ethiopia

How can charities raise funds and ensure that they present an accurate and balanced picture of the situation?

The guidelines of Save the Children

- The dignity of people should be preserved.
- The images and text must be accurate.
- People should be seen as active and not just recipients of aid.
- Disabled people are an active part of the community and should be seen that way.
- Patronizing, sentimental or demeaning words or phrases should be avoided.
- Attempts should be made where possible to identify and quote people being photographed or interviewed.
- Text and photographs which contradict or present conflicting messages should be avoided.

Case study

The Royal National Institute for the Blind (RNIB) is one of the largest charities in the UK, working with people who have sight problems. In 1993 the RNIB introduced a new logo, shown here, as it was felt that the old logo reinforced the idea among the public that people with sight problems were helpless, miserable, and could do nothing for themselves.

Royal National Institute for the Blind

The new RNIB logo.

This of course is far from the case, and the new logo was designed to promote a more positive and optimistic image: the figure, of no particular age or gender, is active and independent. Although the long cane is a universally recognized symbol for blind and partially sighted people, there are no boundaries around the figure, who is striding forward purposefully.

Do charities work?

As we move into the twenty-first century, we have to look again at the role of charity within our society. Should charities continue to exist at all? If so, how do we decide which organizations can be charities? Should charities continue to enjoy tax concessions? What responsibility should the state take for people who are in any kind of need? Will the public continue to support charities? Can charities really make a difference?

Case study

Dom Hélder Câmara was born in Brazil in 1909. He was one of 13 children. From a young age he wanted to be a priest. Câmara achieved his ambition, and in 1964 he became the archbishop of Recife in north-east Brazil.

Câmara's great concern was with the poor people who lived in slums, and much of his work was about trying to help them. He felt that it was wrong for him to live the comfortable and luxurious lifestyle that went with being an archbishop. He moved out of the bishop's palace into a much more humble home and refused to wear a cross made from gold or silver. Instead he wore a cross made from wood.

Câmara believed that charity, in the sense of handing out food and clothing to the poor, was not enough to really help them. He thought that what people needed were social justice and human rights. They should not have to rely on handouts. Society should ensure that its people were not poor in the first place.

Dom Hélder Câmara.

Public support

Although charities use more and more imaginative and 'fun' ways to encourage us to part with our money, the truth is that fewer people now donate to charity, and donations have become smaller. Polls show that public confidence in charities is ebbing. There is a need now for charities to promote themselves as more than just a good cause – they must 'market' themselves.

Câmara believed that no one should have to live in a slum like this.

Dom Hélder Câmara's suggestions about how society could be changed in order to achieve such equality made him unpopular with many people, including the Brazilian government. He received many death threats, and priests who worked with him were murdered as a warning to him.

Câmara retired in 1984, but he is held in worldwide regard, and was nominated for the Nobel Peace Prize as a result of his tireless work.

Charities must shift from seeing themselves as deserving of support because of the need or problem they tackle and begin believing that they earn support by being a good investment. For many charities this represents a complete change in their approach.

Charities have responded to these new pressures by becoming more professional and businesslike. However, this produces a mixed response from the public. Some see it as charities being more efficient and accountable but others feel alienated by what they see as a less human and friendly face.

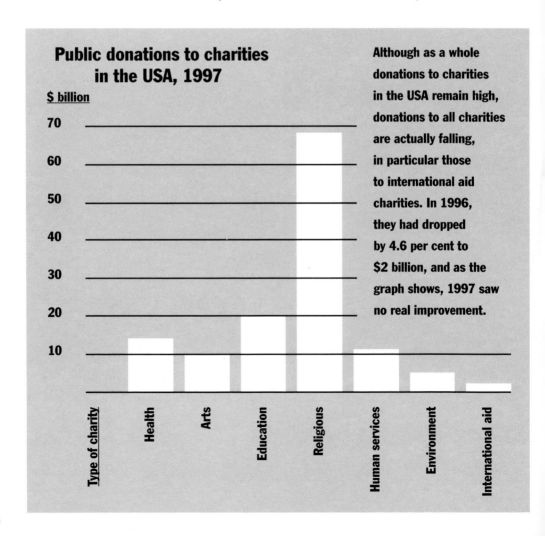

Public donations to charities in the USA, 1997

$ billion

70
60
50
40
30
20
10

Type of charity Health Arts Education Religious Human services Environment International aid

Although as a whole donations to charities in the USA remain high, donations to all charities are actually falling, in particular those to international aid charities. In 1996, they had dropped by 4.6 per cent to $2 billion, and as the graph shows, 1997 saw no real improvement.

Donor fatigue

'Donor fatigue', or 'compassion fatigue', is the idea that we are less interested in charities generally – that we are beginning to develop resistance to the whole idea of charity.

This may be because people feel that their donation will make very little difference. Most of us can only afford to give a very little amount to charity, and how can this possibly change the world? In their advertising and publicity materials, charities are keen to give us details of what just a small amount can do to help individual people. On the other hand, when the scale of the problem is given, donors can feel overwhelmed to the extent that they think it is not worth doing anything.

Another possible reason for donor fatigue is the number of times we are asked to give. Look through any newspaper and you might see several advertisements for the same cause and many others for different causes. We can feel overwhelmed and confused, and think that it is easier not to give to any charity at all.

Whether 'donor fatigue' exists or not is not really proved, but it is nevertheless something about which charities cannot afford to be complacent.

Talking point

'It tends to make the charitable think that he has done his duty by giving away some trifling sum, his conscience is put to sleep and he does not trouble to consider the social problem any further.'

Clement Attlee, British Prime Minister 1945–51 and creator of the welfare state

Do you agree that people just give to charity so that they feel they have done their duty? Do you think people should get more involved?

Donor fatigue may be affecting the amount that people are willing to give to charity.

Charity or business?

In many countries, particularly in the West, the way in which charities work and the type of work they do has changed radically in the last few years. Charities have been drawn into providing a range of services previously assumed to be the responsibility of the state, particularly in the field of social welfare.

They have changed from being small organizations that give help to the needy, and have become large businesslike organizations that take contracts from local government to run, for example, child protection services or day centres for the elderly. In place of fundraising, charities are tendering for contracts. In addition to this, because they are charities they can still receive donations from the public.

Social welfare of this kind has previously been considered to be the responsibility of governments. The United Nations Declaration of Human Rights says that everyone should have the right to a 'standard of living adequate for the health and well-being of himself'. If social welfare of this kind is considered a 'right' then it raises the question of whether it should be left up to

Without the help of Médecins Sans Frontières, this little refugee girl's chances of survival would have been slim, let alone her chances of an adequate standard of living.

On a pedestal

'Charities have been put on a pedestal so long they fail to recognize that the future will be private companies doing it better.'

Mike Edwards, author,
Observer magazine, 1996

charities to provide, or whether governments need to be more responsible for it. Although charities receive government grants for this kind of work, they are also being subsidized by the donations they receive from the public.

Should charities continue to exist?

In an ideal world, most charities would not exist. Everyone would have the right to the things they need to enjoy an independent life. Charities often say that they are working towards the day when their organization will no longer be needed – working towards their own extinction. If we believe that people have a right to a decent standard of living, enough food to eat and somewhere to live, then this should not be left to the whim of individuals who donate to charity.

However, if all charities were done away with tomorrow millions of people would be left worse off. Without charities and without a safety net there could be a return to a situation where there are no measures at all to help the poor and needy. In the short term this is not the answer.

Will the day ever arrive when charities are no longer needed?

Glossary

Activist Someone who follows up their beliefs by taking action and doing something to tackle a problem. Environmental and animal welfare activists are probably the best known.

Almshouse A charitable institution for the poor.

Beneficiary A person who receives help or money from a charity.

Campaign A series of events organized by a charity to inform people about a particular case or issue. Originally a campaign was a term used for part of a military operation.

Civil rights Rights guaranteed by law, to which every citizen is entitled. In the USA the struggle to obtain civil rights for black people was a major feature of the 1960s. Today, many groups representing people with disabilities are campaigning to obtain full civil rights for them.

Community development The idea that in order to improve conditions for people in the long term, the quality of life of whole communities must be improved, giving them a sense of identity and purpose, and 'helping them to help themselves'.

Development agency The name given to a charity that provides aid to poorer countries. Usually, but not always, development agencies have their headquarters in Europe or North America, and run aid programmes in Africa, Asia or South America.

Donation A gift of money or goods to charity.

Dysentery Inflammation of the intestines caused by bacterial infection.

Empowerment The passing on of power to individuals or community groups so that they can take decisions in matters which relate to them, and not have to rely on others.

Funding The financial backing a charity needs in order to run its programme and projects. Funding may come from many different sources, from small private donations to lottery grants or large donations from major companies.

Humanitarian A way of behaving which takes account of the welfare and well-being of other people. Humanitarian organizations are those that work towards improving the condition of the world's poor and disadvantaged.

Industrial Revolution During the nineteenth century this was a period of rapid change in Britain when factories were built and people moved from the countryside to the cities to find work.

Legacy Money or items which are left in a will. This is an increasingly important source of funds for charities.

Lobby Attempt to gain the support of influential people or members of the public in order to influence decisions or policy.

Moonie A member of the Unification Church, a sect founded in 1954 by Sun Myung Moon, who was born in South Korea.

Motor neurone disease A group of disorders in which there is degeneration of the nerves that control muscular activity. This leads to weakness and wasting of the muscles. To date the cause is unknown.

Philanthropist Someone who tries to help other people, usually by giving a lot of money to charity or doing good deeds.

Turnover The amount of money (before tax) earned by a business, usually measured over a year.

Typhoid An infectious bacterial fever that attacks the intestines.

Books to read

A Cause for our Times by Maggie Black (Oxfam, 1992)

Aid in Action by Alistair Ross (A & C Black, 1989)

Helping You, Helping Me by Mog Ball (Michael O'Mara Books, 1990)

Mother Teresa (Life Stories Series) by Wayne Jackson (Wayland, 1993)

Repairing the Damage: Famine and Hunger by Lawrence Williams (Cloverleaf, 1992)

Saving the Children by Brigid Avison (Hamish Hamilton, 1985)

Taking Action! A series published by Heinemann which includes:
Barnardo's
Comic Relief
Greenpeace
Help the Aged
Oxfam
RSPCA
Shelter

The Rich-Poor Divide by Teresa Garlake (Wayland, 1995)

Useful addresses

UK

Carousel
Community Base
113/117 Queens Road
Brighton BN1 3XG
Tel: 01273 234734

Charities Aid Foundation
Kings Hill
West Malling
Kent ME19 4TA
http://www.charitynet.org/
Tel: 01732 520 000

Charity Commission for England and Wales
St Alban's House
57–60 Haymarket
London SW1Y 4QX
Tel: 0171 210 4556

IFAW
Warren Court
Park Road
Crowborough
East Sussex
TN26 2GA

Médecins sans Frontières
124–132 Clerkenwell Road
London EC1R 5DL
http://www.msf.org/

National Council for Voluntary Organizations
Regents Wharf
8 All Saints Street
London N1 9RL

National Eczema Society
163 Evershott Street
London NW1 1BU

Oxfam
274 Banbury Road
Oxford OX2 7DZ
Tel: 01865 311 311

Royal National Institute for the Blind (RNIB)
224 Great Portland Street
London W1N 6AA
http://www.rnib.org.uk/
Tel: 0171 388 8316

Royal Society for the Prevention of Cruelty to
Animals (RSPCA)
Causeway
Horsham
West Sussex RH12 1ZA
http://www.rspca.org.uk/

Save the Children Fund
17 Grove Lane
London SE5 8RD
http://www.oneworld.org/scf/
Tel: 0171 703 5400

The Scottish Council for Voluntary Organizations
18/19 Claremont Crescent
Edinburgh EH7 4RD

Voluntary Service Overseas (VSO)
317 Putney Bridge Road
London SW15 2PN
http://www.oneworld.org/vso/
Tel: 0181 780 2266

USA

American Red Cross
PO Box 37243
Washington DC 20013
http://www.redcross.org/

National Charities Information Bureau
6th Floor
19 Union Street West
New York 10003–3395

Project Hope
Health Sciences Center
Carter Hall
Millwood
VA 22646
http://www.prohope.org/

Salvation Army
PO Box 4269
Alexandria
VA 22313
http://www/salvationarmy.org/

The Philanthropic Advisory Service
4200 Wilson Blvd.
Arlington
VA 22203

Australia

Médecins sans Frontières
Suite C, Level 1
263 Broadway
Glebe
NSW 2037
http://www.msf.org/

RSPCA
PO Box E369
Kingston
ACT 2604

Index

Numbers in **bold** refer to illustrations.